Rambles by Rail

No. 2 Liskeard–Looe

Les Lumsdon

GW00498931

Published by Platform 5 Publishing Limited, Lydgate House, Lydgate Lane, Sheffield S10 5FH

ISBN 1 872524 17 6

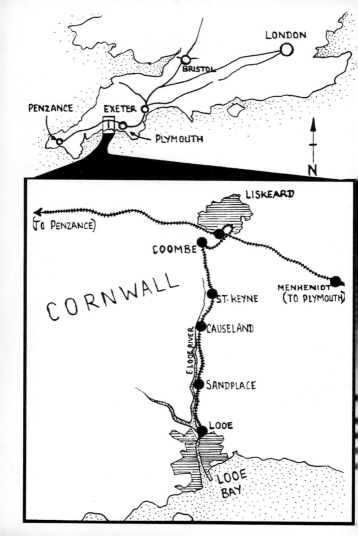

CONTENTS

East meets West 4

Walk 1: Liskeard to Coombe 15

Walk 2: Liskeard to Coombe via Bolitho 19

Walk 3: Coombe to St. Keyne 23

Walk 4: St. Keyne Circular Ramble 27

Walk 5: St. Keyne to Looe 29

Walk 6: St. Keyne to Causeland via Landlooe Bridge 37

Walk 7: St. Keyne to Causeland by way of Herodsfoot ... 39

Walk 8: St. Keyne to Sandplace via Trewidland 45

Walk 9: Causeland to Sandplace by road 49

Walk 10: Causeland to Looe by way of Pelynt 51

Walk 11: Causeland to Sandplace by way of Duloe 57

Walk 12: Sandplace to Looe by way of the

West Looe Valley 59

Walk 13: Sandplace to Morval Circular Ramble 61

Walk 14: Sandplace to Ringworthy Circular Ramble 63

Walk 15: Polperro to Looe 67

Walk 16: Looe to Talland Bay Circular Ramble 71

Walk 17: Looe to Kilminorth 75

A brief History 77

Please note that all photographs in this book are taken by Les Lumsdon.

EAST MEETS WEST

Where the East and West Looe rivers meet stands the terminus of one of Britain's finest scenic branch lines, the Liskeard to Looe railway. The 8¾ mile journey from Liskeard takes a little over half an hour to reach the station of Looe, tucked away on the edge of town on a shoulder of the river. It is as well that the train does saunter through the East Looe valley for the wildlife is so visible. It is possible to see kingfishers and dragonflies on the upper river and the Grey Heron and dozens of wader birds on the estuary at low tide. What better introduction to this secluded part of East Cornwall?

Looe

An author of a much earlier walks book stated that one's arrival in Looe is always a matter for self congratulation! It is uncertain in the context whether he was telling the reader something about his rambles or about finding this most attractive of Cornish resorts. It has always, no doubt, been a place of natural beauty but its status as a resort has come late in its existence.

Seafaring

The harbour is of considerable antiquity and for centuries the compact settlements of East and West Looe have both enjoyed a seafaring existence, so much so that at times of war they were called upon to provide men and ships way above what would have been expected elsewhere. The Looe Town Trail guide, an absolute must to purchase, tells of the towns of Looe supplying 325 men and 20 ships for Edward III at the Seige of Calais. Can you imagine the port brimming to the full with sea going sailing vessels; men aboard ready to set sail?

Ancient Highways

It doesn't take long to figure the reason why East and West Looe grew up here at the bridging point of this sheltered estuary. Not only did the sea bring trade but we must also look to the ancient highways from Plymouth and Penzance. Looe would have been a natural place to rest a while before continuing overland to a final destination. Needless to say, considering the amount of trade it is surprising that the two communities have stayed so far apart, so independent of each other. In Civic terms this has certainly been the case. For until the Great Reform Act of 1832 both East and West Looe returned two representatives to Parliament.

Revived Fortunes

Two major economic activities in this part of Cornwall revived the fortunes of Looe harbour in the nineteenth century. The first was the drive by local landowners to enclose and improve their fields for agricultural purposes. Lime and sand were transported inwards and crops outward. Secondly and perhaps more importantly, the extraction of minerals, principally copper but also tin, stimulated an enormous amount of trade if on an erratic basis. Thus, the port became less well known for its pilchards and more as a port for exporting copper, tin and granite as well.

Transhipment

Hence, the development of the canal between Moorswater and Terras Bridge and following this the building of a railway to cope with heavier and more regular flows of minerals. This brought about a change to Looe. The quayside not only coped with a fishing fleet but also larger vessels burgeoning with copper ore. Transhipment would have taken place where children now go crabbing and there would have been piles of ore, slabs of granite and rail wagons where people now park their cars by the bridge.

A fisherman prepares the daily catch for sale in Looe
Harbour.

Tourism

Tourism played a small part only in the development of Looe prior to the nineteenth century. There would have always been travellers with their wagons and packhorses passing through, foreign sailors in town, and later in the nineteenth century the genteel urban traveller seeking a respite from the grime and filth of the rapidly expanding towns but the numbers would not have been significant. In fact Looe beach began to be seen more as an attraction after the Napoleonic Wars and there was even a bathing machine installed. This, however, appears to have not gone down too well and soon fell into disrepair.

Railway

It was the railway that brought mass tourism to Looe. This was particularly so when train travel became cheaper and people of all social classes began to escape the cities for a day or a week at the seaside. The large railway companies such as The Great Western Railway promoted travel to Cornwall in a way that the country had never seen before and thus the economy of Looe had transformed once again within 30 years of the complete collapse of tin mining during the latter decades of the last century.

Fishing

The survivor has been fishing and what a brave initiative the authorities made when allowing the newly-built fish market to stand where copper and granite would have been stock piled a hundred years ago. This gives Looe a sense of real identity, with fish being brought in on the tide by the thirty to forty working trawlers based at Looe harbour. It adds life to the town. Resident and visitor alike sit back to watch a boat or two arrive with a catch whatever the time of day or night.

The old toll house in the quiet West Looe.

Sharks

For those who enjoy the sport of fishing this must be a paradise. It is the headquarters of shark fishing in the UK and whatever your fancy there is always a boat willing to take a small party out into the Channel in search of a shoal or two. The rest of us are content to take the more sedate trip around St George's Island or even settle for the one minute journey across the quay by ferry. The ferrymen add so much character to the place. These good humoured weatherworn mariners provide a friendly service when tides permit and no visit to Looe is complete without a trip between East and West Looe.

East Looe

The towns are not without interest. East Looe is crammed full with narrow ways and passages. No manner of commercialism can spoil this and once off the main throroughfare the streets are far quieter with the occasional cafe or restaurant enticing the passer-by indoors. The layout of the town means that cars have been kept out, a Godsend to the pedestrian. There is 'access only' throughout much of the old town, the major car park being on the old mill pond site across the bridge.

For lovers of local history a visit to The Guildhall, dating from the early 1500s, is not to be missed. The outer stair way leads to the one time Council chamber and Court House. Further along Higher Market Street is the beach, with a front that is none too exciting. The beach, however, is clean, safe and dogs are not allowed. Adjacent is Banjo Pier, named after its unusual shape and is an ideal place to be to watch the boats bob in and out of the harbour.

West Looe

West Looe is quieter. It has two interesting squares, West Looe Square which is where buses turn and beyond it is Princes Square surrounded by interesting buildings dating from different times. In the centre is the old market house, built in 1853, hexagonal in format and with a bell turret. It stands today as a florist and grocery shop. There are steps up to West Looe Downs from near here with great views across the harbour to the sea.

Countryside

What makes Looe so interesting is the surrounding beautiful countryside within ten minutes walk from the town. Both the East and West Looe river valleys are quiet haunts not much frequented by locals or visitors. They are very sparsely populated farming areas now with a smattering of farm cottages converted for holiday use.

Green Lanes

The paths in the West Looe valley are reasonably well used. Cornwall County Council has carried out remedial work on the routes such as re-stiling and providing sign posting at key points. They have also produced a leaflet outlining a ramble between Liskeard and Looe which should be available in local libraries and Tourist Information Centres. The East Looe valley is less well endowed with paths and while open there are fewer signs and stiles to assist the rambler. Nevertheless, the green lanes are a saviour to the walker. These often bear the status of county council highways but are mainly used only by walkers and horse riders. They are rich in wildlife, provide good views as they dip into the deep sided river valleys and are for the most part car free.

Rail Rambles

Why use the train to enjoy these walks? There are several good reasons. The train penetrates parts of the East Looe valley which are hard to get to by car. In fact, the limited and narrow road network has probably been the saviour of the line. When Dr Beeching proposed sweeping rail closures there was a question mark about this one because it would have been impossible to mirror the route by replacement bus.

By using the train you are helping to keep a line open for local people and on your travels you will find that the train stops to take country people to work or the shops albeit in small numbers. Furthermore, the car is a real intrusion down back lanes where no proper car parking exists. More cars would destroy the very tranquillity that exists in these parts. Using the train allows a gentle, more sustainable approach to enjoying the Cornish countryside.

Good Fun

More importantly, it is simply good fun. There are so many querks about the line. From Liskeard onwards unaware passengers are baffled when the train leaves from a platform which is at right angles to the main station, curves sharply under the Plymouth to Penzance line and then reverses down the line to Looe! Open the window at St Keyne station and the sound of music drifts into the carriage for Mr Corin's Magical Music Machines are housed within metres of the platform. The station at Causeland is tended by a local Farm holiday company and often the people at The West Looe Valley Crafts in Sandplace give a wave to the train when they're serving teas in the garden. It is that sort of line. The train crew have time to be friendly and many of the conductor guards are very knowledgeable about both the history and wildlife along the branch. The pace is right to enjoy yourselves.

Remember that Coombe Junction, St Keyne and Sandplace are request stops so tell the guard well before if you want to alight at any of these and make a hand signal if you wish the train to stop to pick you up. No need to wave frantically, the driver usually hoots when he has spotted you. Don't be anxious as the crews are on the look out for passengers! More often than not, however, they are at each station on the dot so don't leave it too late. A sit down for five or ten minutes after a ramble is ideal before the arrival of the train.

The Walks

The walks are varied. Most include road walking for part of a walk and in one or two instances for most of the route. In other parts of England this would be a real disadvantage but here the steep sided, centuries old, back lanes are rich in flowers and carry very few cars. They are a joy to walk. Most of the paths are clear. However, in places the way might be less easy to follow, with stiles and gates being old and paths not so well walked. They can be a little off-putting to the casual walker who does not venture into the countryside on a regular basis. Hopefully, improvements will occur on these sections in the near future but in the meantime do not be put off. They are rights of way and we are entitled to walk along them from one point to another without hindrance.

Easier Routes

If you are less easy about these try the more popular walks first such as Walks 1, 3, 4, 9 and 15. Then try one of the harder routes. Sometimes, in the Spring when the vegetation becomes lush, paths can begin to become overgrown in places. Take or pick up a stick for these sections.

Liskeard to Looe

By combining Walks 1, 3 and 5 there is a long but superbly rewarding ramble from Liskeard through to Looe mainly following the lie of the land from market town to seaside resort. There are, after all, cut off points prior to St Keyne station. Other combinations can be worked out such a Coombe Junction to Sandplace, for example.

Clothing

Most of the walks can be enjoyed without having special outdoor clothing. In the summer, trainers can be as comfortable as boots. After wet weather, however, the paths will be muddy and where dairy farms exist there is always a churning up of paths leading to the dairy. At all times take something water proof for if the weather does turn unkind it can get chilly if you get wet to the skin. If walking in other seasons warm and waterproof outdoor clothing is essential.

The walks are described in reasonable detail so this book is all you require to successfully complete a mission. The directions are always listed as if you have your back to a stile or building as such. For example, if you have just crossed a stile and the instruction reads 'Proceed slightly right up the hill' this would mean with your back to the stile, start walking slightly to the right across the field. Inevitably things change and we apologise in advance for imponderables such as trees being planted where sheep once grazed or where a previously described derelict barn has become a restored holiday cottage.

Crops

The planting of crops without re-instating a path can be a problem for the rambler. Farmers should always re-instate the line of a path if a crop is planted in any particular field. You have a right to continue across the field in the line of the path. Some people feel more comfortable, however, walking around the edge to regain the true line in the next field. If a path is obstructed by barbed wire or any other material you are entitled to remove the obstruction to get by or to take a feasible route around the blockage and then rejoin your path. If this occurs please let Cornwall County Council know or write to the publisher who will pass on the details. In fact, if you have any comments to improve the book let the publisher know so that others may gain from our collective experience.

Local Shops

Don't forget to follow the Country Code and above all else enjoy your rail rambles. There are not so many pubs and tea rooms on routes but the ones you will come across are most enjoyable. There are also village shops where drinks and food can be obtained. Use them whenever you can for the extra revenue from us often helps the village store or post office to survive. It allows us to plough something back into these local communities which make the walks so attractive.

Enjoy Your Walking

The East and West Looe valleys are beautiful parts of the South West not much traversed by the walker and the Looe branch is a splendid railway worthy of our support, whatever the season. Combine the two and you are bound to have fun in this very special part of Cornwall. Enjoy your walking.

Swans on the Looe Estuary.

LISKEARD TO COOMBE

Liskeard station is on the south western side of town, a 7 to 8 minute walk from the town centre. The ramble allows the walker to explore this old town, including its Town Museum, before dipping into the surrounding countryside, passing Ladye Park and walking beneath the very distinctive Moorswater Viaduct. A final stretch alongside the old canal leads to Coombe Junction station.

The walk is partly on roads, partly on paths which are obvious, waymarked along one section and easy to follow.

From Liskeard railway station turn right into Station Road by The Tavern An Carow and walk into town along the main thoroughfare which takes several names – Barn Street, Barras Street and then The Parade.

Old-Fashioned

Liskeard is, in many respects, an old-fashioned town. It has retained its sense of independence from Plymouth, is not overawed by the flow of tourists travelling further west and has a strong market town feel despite its mining heritage. Throughout the centuries Liskeard has prospered although there have been times of depression, particularly after the decline of the copper mining during the last century.

Stannary Town

The area surrounding the town had been mined for copper and tin for centuries and the importance of this was recognised when it became chartered as a stannary town in 1307 joining Bodmin, Helston, Lostwithiel and Truro. All tin produced in the locality had to be brought to Liskeard for testing of purity and taxation purposes. This and other fascinating aspects of the town's history are displayed in The Town Museum which you pass shortly. There's also a characterful book about the town 'Liskeard Town and

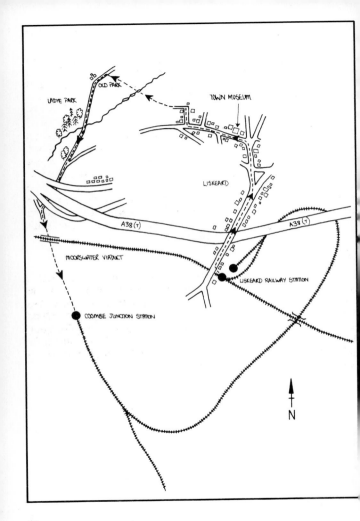

16

About' by Peter Moore and Martin Lister available in local bookshops.

At the top of The Parade, turn left into West Street, and walk by The Town Museum on your right. Follow this road for less than half a mile, looking for a dark, tree-covered lane on your right which is signed as a path.

Old Park

This lane curves left to a stile which you cross and shortly afterwards another is reached. Once over this go right down the hill, with the hedge on your right until you reach yet another stile. Climb this and head slightly left to the stream, which is a tributary of the East Looe River. Cross the bridge and another stile beyond, then follow the fence on the left up the field to the right of Old Park, a solid Georgian building overlooking this gentle valley. The path exits onto a minor road where you turn left.

Ladye Park

This delightful back lane passes Ladye Park on the right, said to be a place of pilgrimage in medieval times, and the site of a former chapel. The lane comes to a junction. Go right and walk under the bypass before turning left. Once past the cottages, turn left again following a track alongside the old lime kilns at Moorswater, remnants belonging to a time when the Liskeard to Looe canal served this early industrial zone.

A branch train arrives at Liskeard from Looe.

WALK TWO: Approximately 3 miles (5 km)

LISKEARD TO COOMBE
via Bolitho

This is a hilly walk with a number of climbs. It leads through town at first, between housing and then across the busy bypass road. From there onwards it follows field paths and quiet lanes to the East Looe valley. The rights of way are not clear in places and therefore care is needed in picking your way along one or two sections.

There are compensations – the views are exquisite and, beyond the main road, it is a very quiet part of Liskeard.

From Liskeard station turn right into Station Road by the Tavern An Carrow. Follow this, as in Walk One towards town and pass by Merlin Glass in Barn Street. At Windsor Place go right along Bay Tree Hill and then right again down the hill. Just past the supermarket turn right again and at the junction by the car park take the narrow lane ahead. This is Sun Girt Lane, a quiet corner devoid of cars. This curves left and look out for a footpath crossing. Go right here for a few paces to modern housing where you cross Meadow Lane and continue ahead between houses to a stile.

Pass By With Care

Believe it or not this leads up to the bypass, virtually built to motorway standards but thankfully far less busy. Take great care nevertheless. Cross to the central reservation, then over the other carriageway to the barrier. At this point you will see a path sloping down left to the culvert and then right to a stile leading into the field. As you begin to breathe again you are no doubt left with the feeling that scant regard has been made for pedestrians here. The railway line to your right is the loop down to Coombe Junction and the viaduct beyond carries the main line.

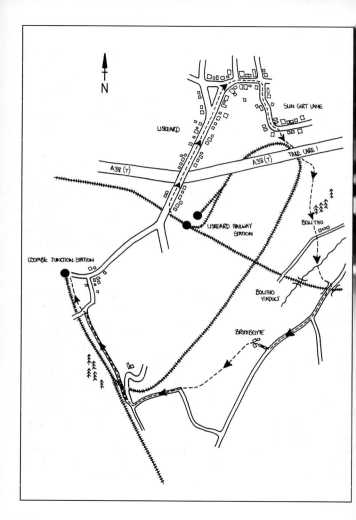

Crescent Shaped Woodland

The Pathfinder map shows a route through the crescent-shaped and fenced woodland ahead. This is not possible so most walkers simply walk slightly right up the bank to go through the gateway and then go left, following the hedge to a gateway on the left. Go through this and keep ahead on the old track leading to the farm buildings. Go through the farmyard and turn right at the lane. This is Bolitho.

Bolitho

Walk a short distance towards the distinguished looking farm, through a gateway, and then go left before the low-level barn on the left. The old track twists right and then left down an old wooded sunken lane. Do not attempt this as it is obstructed with scrub and rubbish. Your nearest alternative is to continue down the field to a gateway which you go through and then left through another and across a bridge.

Bolitho Viaduct

In the next field go slightly right up the steep hillside, stepping up the ripples of soil creep brought about by rainwater seeping below the surface for centuries. The view of Bolitho Viaduct is very rewarding. The way in which the engineers, under Isambard Kingdom Brunel, designed the Plymouth to Truro railway meant that so many of these viaducts crossed valley landscapes thereby offering glimpses of the countryside to passengers travelling to their holiday destinations. With the medium of local stone and splendid arching the viaducts almost look part of the natural environment. The farming community at the time, however, were most disturbed by such construction work and fear was that the rumble of fiery engines through peaceful dairy pastures would bring ruin to their herds. The cows now seem to take little heed of the up express to London.

Views Into The Valley

Climb up to the gateway which has a gate of sorts, and once over go right along the field edge to come alongside the railway and then left to a minor road. Go right, over the railway and at the next junction keep ahead. Shortly afterwards, look for a lane leading off right through two small pillars. The farm track passes a bungalow on the right and then curves left to approach Brimboyte farmhouse. The track bears right and then left between outbuildings and within a few paces look for a gateway on the right. Go through it and turn left. Keep alongside the hedge to the field corner where you climb over stone steps. In the next field go slightly right to a gateway which you go through. There are good views into the East Looe Valley across this field.

Turn right onto the back lane and this leads down by cottages to the B3254 beneath Lodge Hill. Go right, left and then right at the junction following the minor road passing under the line linking Liskeard with Coombe Junction. Coombe Junction station is signed left off this lane, through a white gate adjacent to Lower Coombe crossing. The quiet halt of Coombe Junction lies just beyond.

COOMBE TO ST KEYNE

This is easy walking, but with two climbs to take at a gentle pace. The route follows minor roads between the two stations of Coombe Junction and St Keyne. These lanes, rich in wildlife and flowers make walking on tarmac far more enjoyable than usual especially as there is little or no traffic. It allows the walker an opportunity to extend Walk One to the rural halt at St Keyne.

From Coombe Junction station, with your back to the Moorswater viaduct, leave by way of the white gate at Lower Coombe crossing. Go left and at the junction immediately beyond turn right. Before walking very far along this lane look for a stile on your left, opposite a clearing on the other side of the road. Go over the stile and walk slightly right up the steep bank of this narrow meadow. Come to a stile in the top left hand corner of the field and once over go right along a track to the B3254 at Lodge Hill.

Lodge Hill

Go right and follow the road down to the bridge over the railway, with fine views either side of the steep incline beneath. Proceed ahead to another bridge over a stream. After this go left by the cottage. This deeply set lane climbs steeply and then winds its way through the old farmstead at Housey. Go right here and the lane dips to pass Great Gormelick and then descends to the East Looe valley bottom once again.

Campion and Foxglove

The hedgerows of these ancient lanes are a haven for wildlife, having been home to a variety of species for centuries and being partly sheltered from modern farming

23

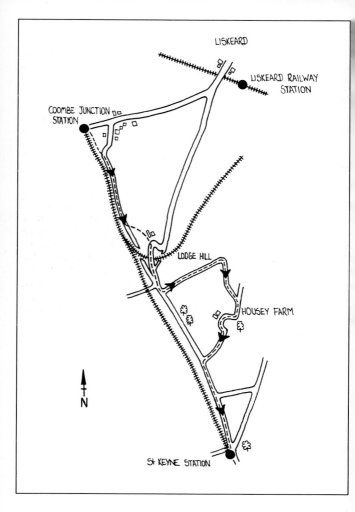

methods. The richness makes walking on tarmac far more enjoyable than in other areas of Britain. With Red Campion, Foxglove and Vetch as bright companions in the hedgerow we become increasingly aware of the importance of the lanes as places where wild flowers can flourish.

To St Keyne

At the junction go left and follow this level road alongside the railway and river for just over half a mile to meet another road coming in from the left. Go right and around the corner go right over the bridge to gain access to the platform of St Keyne station.

Magnificent Musical Machines

Just beyond is Paul Corin's Magnificent Music Machines, a most unusual attraction in a most unlikely setting. There are a number of music making machines from the earlier part of the century including a 1910 German Carousel Organ, a 1929 Mighty Wurlitzer Theatre Pipe Organ and a host of other nostalgic exhibits which have been lovingly restored. As you stand on St Keyne station the music drifts across from the exhibition halls and passengers boarding the train can be forgiven for humming a tune or tapping their feet!

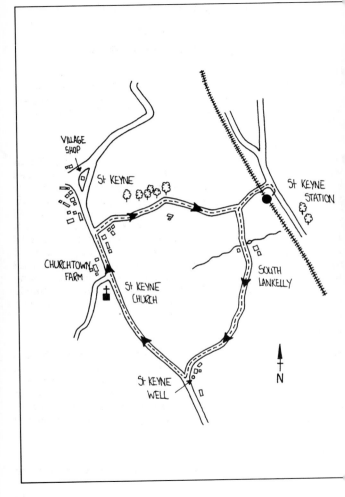

VILLAGE SHOP

St KEYNE

St KEYNE STATION

CHURCHTOWN FARM

St KEYNE CHURCH

SOUTH LANKELLY

St KEYNE WELL

N

WALK FOUR: Approximately 2 miles (3 km)

ST KEYNE
CIRCULAR RAMBLE

This short ramble along quiet lanes to St Keyne's Well and St Keyne village is easy walking with one main climb out of the railway station. Combined with a visit to Paul Corin's Magnificent Music Machines it makes for a lovely morning or afternoon outing.

St Keyne's Well

From St Keyne station turn left and pass by the Magnificent Music Machines in and around the old mill. Follow the road around to the left and continue ahead up the hill for over half a mile to St Keyne's Well. This tree covered well, restored by the Old Cornwall Society in 1936, is still something of a mystery and charm. A slate monument tells the tale but in case your eyesight is not strong the gist of the yarn is as follows. St Keyne was a 6th century saint of great strength and purity who travelled throughout the land before settling in this part of Cornwall. According to legend she blessed the waters of this well so that when a couple came to drink them the partner to sip first would gain mastery throughout the marriage.

A Taste of Power

Your sigh of disbelief would not have been accepted by the Victorians for it was evidently a very well established custom for newly weds to race down from the village to the well to see who tasted the waters first however undignified the episode became. Couples still turn up to put the legend to the test but please remember fighting is not allowed in the environs of the well.

St Keyne Village

At the junction by the well go right and follow the lane to

St Keyne church which appears on the left. Keep ahead in the village and, unless you intend to call into the village shop further up the road, go right by The Chapel Bakery to return down the narrow lane to the railway station, bearing left at the junction at the bottom of the hill.

St. Keyne Church.

WALK FIVE: Approximately 11 miles (18 km)

ST KEYNE TO LOOE

This is the longest ramble in the book so it is worth setting aside the best part of the day for the journey down the West Looe valley along paths and tracks which weave in and around this beautiful river. There are no inns on the route so a picnic is essential although there are village stores at St Keyne and Herodsfoot.

There are a few steep climbs but for the most part the gradients are gentle and tracks and paths obvious. The first part of the walk to St Keyne's Well is as described in Walk Four.

Start from St Keyne station. Go left and at the junction beyond Paul Corins Magical Musical Machines keep left and make your way up to St Keyne's Well. The story of this lovely old well is told in Walk Four but it suffices to say that the battle of the sexes continues in local custom and legend.

Abundance of Kisses

At the road junction by the well turn right and follow this road up the short rise where you will see two gateways on the left. Walk through the kissing gate alongside the second gate. Please remember the old custom of kissing the person behind you, depending on who it is, of course! Keep company with the hedge on your right as you proceed to another kissing gate, the landowner here obviously being keen on this type of access and it does seem to work well for both the farmer and walker. Go through the gate and then walk slightly right to a gateway by the tree cover. You will catch a glimpse of St Keyne church in the foreground and Liskeard in the background.

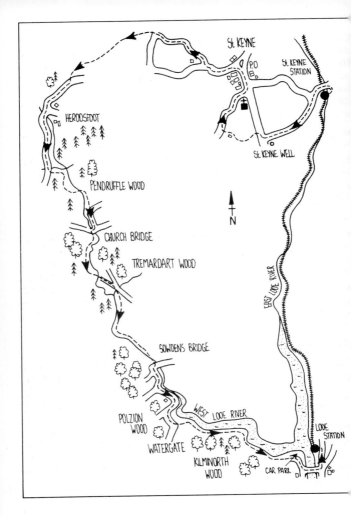

30

St Keyne Church

Go through the kissing gate and walk ahead for a short distance to a junction of paths. Go left, passing by The Old Rectory Country House hotel and then right down the access road to the B3254. Go right and walk along the road for a short distance to St Keyne. Beware of traffic. The church is an austere looking building standing at the southern end of the village.

Walk through the village with the Chapel Bakery on the right and then take the next main junction left and left again heading now towards Herodsfoot. However, not far out of the village after the road curves right by East Trevillies and then left, go right up a track by West Trevillies.

Good Views

This green lane climbs gently, offering good views of the surrounding countryside, then dips to a main road. Cross this and go through the gateway as signed. Head for the top left hand corner of the field, go through the gateway, and continue ahead through the next field to another gateway. Keep ahead, following the field edge but being vigilant in looking for a step stile over the hedge before the field begins to curve right.

West Looe Ahead

Cross the stile and turn slightly right, following the left hand hedge down the field to another gateway in the left hand corner. Go through it and continue ahead to cross a stile. The views into The West Looe valley begin to open up across to Liggars and Porlphar Woods. Once again, follow the boundary down the field and go through the gateway on the left which brings you into the adjacent field. Head for the far right hand corner and be prepared to drop, almost literally down the stone steps to the lane below. Go right for Herodsfoot.

Mining Heritage

As the lane descends you will see the chimney of one of Herodsfoot's lead mines. Can you believe that this tranquil corner was once a thriving tin mining area during the mid 19th century ? There had been smaller mines in the area from the early 18th century, but the larger mine to the south was established in the 1840s during the boom period. There was also a gunpowder factory in the vicinity.

Woodworm in The Pump

Walk by the old water pump, with the initials JLR on it and a painted surround complete with woodworm. Meet another road coming in from the left and continue right into the village, passing by the village shop and post office. The road crosses the river and climbs away into woodland. In about half a mile, after crossing a bridge over a tributary brook turn left into Pendruffle Wood on a forestry track.

Church Bridge

Follow this for a short distance, looking out for a turning left over a large footbridge and then a smaller one before turning right. The path follows an old mill leat which, in earlier times, carried water down to the nearby mill. Then climb up to a forestry track which then leads ahead to a minor road. Go right here, passing the old mill and coming upon the lovely Church Bridge.

Tremardart Wood

Turn left after the bridge into woodland once again and follow this forestry track through to an opening in approximately three quarters of a mile where you turn left to cross the bridge and then follow the main green lane upward above a flood plain by the river. This meets another lane coming in from the left (as mentioned in WALK TEN) and descends to a ford. You, however, turn left over the sleeper footbridge, cross the stile and go slightly right through the

...he stone steps which lead to a sunken lane near Herodsfoot.

meadow above the marshy ground festooned with yellow irises. Some walk to the left of the old hedge, some to the right. Either way it leads into woodland, once again, by way of a stile.

St Nonna's Well

On the other side of the valley you may well have seen a farm and a new access road to it. Near this lies an ancient well known as St Nonna's or Ninnie's or even Piskies Well. This well is surrounded in mystery. One story tells of a local greedy farmer who cast covetous eyes on the well's granite basin to use in his pig sty. He drove oxen to the well and try as he may he could not unsettle the basin. Indeed, retribution struck swiftly. The oxen fell dead on the spot and the farmer became lame and speechless. Seems a little excessive but there we are. On a far more pleasant note those who drop a small pin into the well are to be blessed with good luck. Perhaps, the Piskies use the pins for what purpose we should not guess.

Sowden's Bridge

Keep to the higher path which drops slightly to pass beneath an old foresters hut and then climbs up steps to descend once again to a tributary stream. This path is shown on the Pathfinder map as being higher up across the field but Cornwall County Council has waymarked a far more acceptable route and this is the way we take, although there are fallen trees to contend with from time to time! Before the stream the path turns left, crosses a footbridge on the right and then another stile before heading gently south again through the woods to Sowden's Bridge.

Kilminorth Woods

Turn right, cross the bridge and follow the road to the left keeping left at the next two junctions, walking between Polzion Wood and the West Looe which is tidal from hereon. The road soon reaches Watergate where you turn

34

eft by Harescombe Lodge into Kilminorth Wood.

This delightful path follows a line above the West Looe River and as it bends near to the boatyard go right up to junction and then down steep steps to the right of the building. Turn right and follow the lane back to the main ar park area at The Mill Pond. The perimeter path by the iver is the interesting although tread daintily in places for his is where several dog owners bring their pets for walkies.

This eventually leads to the shops and cafes by the bridge. Cross the bridge and go left for Looe station. There's always The Globe public house opposite the station entrance should ou wish to quench a thirst after your ramble!

e old pump at Herodsfoot.

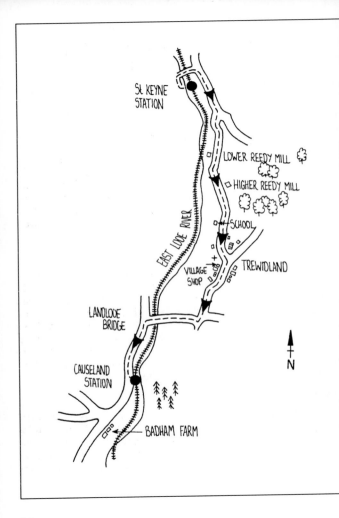

St KEYNE STATION

LOWER REEDY MILL

HIGHER REEDY MILL

EAST LOOE RIVER

SCHOOL

TREWIDLAND

VILLAGE SHOP

LANDLOOE BRIDGE

CAUSELAND STATION

BADHAM FARM

N

WALK SIX: Approximately 2 miles (3 km)

ST KEYNE TO CAUSELAND
via Landlooe Bridge

This short walk between the stations of St Keyne and Causeland is easy going but with climbs, however. The views from Trewidland up the West Looe valley are splendid.

From St Keyne station turn right and right again along the road. At the fork take the right hand turn and follow this lane past an old mill, known appropriately as Lower Reedy Mill and then up to Trewidland school. The views back up the valley are exceptional so take a break and admire them. The road, however, continues to rise steeply up to the village of Trewidland and into a pleasant street known as The Village. Turn right and pass by the village shop, local chapels and village hall.

Landlooe Bridge

The road descends to a junction. Keep right and follow it down to Landlooe Bridge where it crosses the railway, old canal bed and river. Looking over the bridge one can imagine what it would have been like if the canal had remained rather than the railway. The canal would have been less functional but most probably prettier and kinder to wildlife than the clearance of the permanent way for the train. At the next junction go left and walk the short distance to Causeland station on the left.

Causeland Station

This small platform in such an isolated place has a colourful planted area tended by the nearby Badham Farm holiday company. Badham farm is two minutes walk from the station and usually has a sign up indicating light refreshments and afternoon teas. This is very much the heartland of the East Looe valley.

A branch line train arrives at Causeland Halt

38

WALK SEVEN: Approximately 8 miles (13 km)

ST KEYNE TO CAUSELAND
by way of Herodsfoot

This route into the West Looe valley is different to that described in Walk Five. It initially follows roads to Herodsfoot, then a woodland footpath up to Carglonnon Farm, returning by way of roads to the village of Duloe and to Causeland through fields. It is an interesting circular walk with several climbs rewarded by good views.

There are village shops in St Keyne, Herodsfoot and Duloe. The latter village has an inn offering light refreshments.

Start at St Keyne station. Turn left to pass by Paul Corin's Magnificent Musical Machines and within a few paces turn right at the junction. Follow this steep and narrow lane up to St Keyne village coming out onto the main road by the chapel bakery. Go right and then left at the main junction. Turn left again passing by the bus shelter and follow this road for about a mile to a main road. Go left and then second right along another lane which soon begins to descend into the hamlet of Herodsfoot.

Herodsfoot

Pass by the chapel and to a junction where you keep ahead for a short distance before going left along a track, which is signed, before the post office. Pass by the old Zion chapel and Millcombe, now private residences. The path crosses a sleeper bridge and into the wood. Take the higher path which curves left uphill and becomes a sunken lane. This curves right and comes to a stile which you cross. Once in the field, go ahead as signed and then turn right before the gateway onto a track between the field and wood.

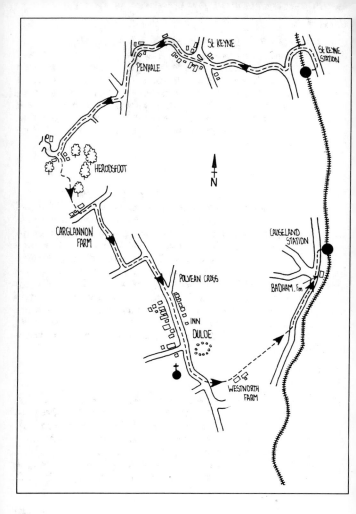

Carglonnon

Go through the gateway and keep ahead for a short distance, going left through the gateway on your left and then head across the next field towards the left hand side of the barn. Your route through Carglonnon Farm is waymarked and please be considerate. Go through two gateways, then left by the milking parlour and pass to the right of the farmhouse. Walk along the drive to a junction where you go left up the tarmac lane to another junction where you turn right.

Duloe Stone Circle

Follow this quiet lane to another T junction where you keep left and in a short while meet a main road. Go right and proceed into Duloe village by way of Polvean Cross. Pass the old water trough, which would be of little use to animals now, and onto Ye Old Plough public house. Continue ahead, if not stopping, and shortly on your left is a turning for the Duloe Stone Circle. It is very well worth a two minute detour. This is a relatively small circle with eight upright quartz stones, a reminder of our prehistoric ancestors and an incredible achievement in making their mark on the landscape. Duloe must have been a settlement of importance even though many of the tribes would have been nomadic in Celtic times.

Duloe Church

Retrace your steps to the main road and continue left towards the church, a solid structure with an impressive 13th century tower. The residents must have welcomed this sanctuary when marauders from afar came to visit. Opposite the turning to The Green are steps over the wall and to your path which is signed. As you walk this section you will see a hotel in the near distance to your right. By this

Duloe Stone Circle.

is St Cuby's Well, one of the ancient wells which characterise Cornwall and at one time was adorned with dolphins and a griffin.

Westnorth Farm

Go slightly right across the field to a gateway which you go through. In the next small field go slightly right to a stile in a hedge adjacent to a trickle of a stream. Cross both and turn right to head towards Westnorth Farm. Go through the gateway and head for the barn to the left of the farmhouse. Go through the gateway and ahead to the next. After going through turn left up to another gateway. This section can get very muddy in wet weather as it is a dairy farm but some ramblers use the narrow path on the left of the enclosure by the farm buildings to avoid the worst.

East Looe Valley

Go through the gateway and walk slightly left to another gate which you pass through. The views into the East Looe valley are good here. Follow the hedge on the left down the field to a gap. Go through it and keep ahead, once again, to a point in the hedge on the left where the old gate has been been broken down and filled by brushwood. Cross this and then go right down hill to the gateway in the bottom left corner of the field.

Turn left on the minor road and follow this by Badham Farm Holidays to Causeland station which is on the right shortly afterwards so completing a fine walk across the watershed of the two river valleys.

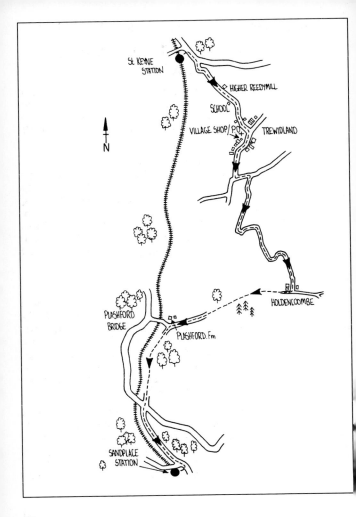

St KEYNE
STATION

HIGHER REEDYMILL

SCHOOL

VILLAGE SHOP / PO

TREWIDLAND

N

HOLDENCOOMBE

PLASHFORD
BRIDGE

PLASHFORD. Fm

SANDPLACE
STATION

44

ST KEYNE TO SANDPLACE
via Trewidland

This walk is along roads mainly but with a delightful green lane in the latter section towards Sandplace from Holdencoombe onwards. It is easy to follow but hilly so take it at a pace to suit. The Walk follows the same route as Walk Six to Trewidland.

From St Keyne station turn right and right again along the road. Within a short distance take the right hand fork for Trewidland, passing by Lower and Higher Reedy Mills, now private houses and then by the local school. The views up the East Looe valley begin to open up as the climb to the village of Trewidland continues. This isolated village with post office, chapel, village institute but no public house in sight, sits high above the Looe valley in the midst of rich farming land.

Plashford Bridge

Go right at the end of the village and follow the lane through the village. At the next junction, beyond the houses, turn left and then very shortly right. The road dips at first then climbs ferociously to a ridge. Keep right at the next junction with the road descending equally fiercely and after the second house at the bottom of the hill at Holdencoombe, turn right along an old green lane which follows a brook down towards Plashford Bridge.

Virtually opposite Plashford Farm take the left hand lane through the woodland and you eventually pass a barricade of corrugated iron on your left before reaching the minor road. Go ahead and at the junction take the lower road. Proceed to the next junction and turn left into Sandplace. The station is on your right, a fine setting for a rural country halt.

Gnomes for sale at Sandplace Old Post Office.

The old lime kiln at Sandplace.

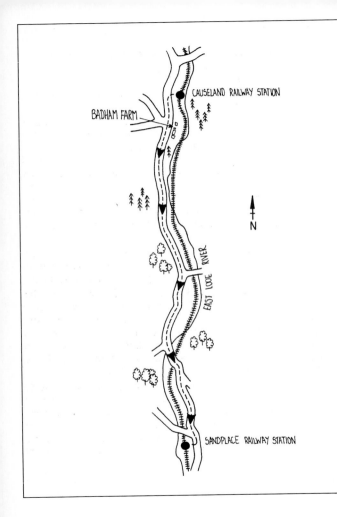

CAUSELAND RAILWAY STATION

BADHAM FARM

EAST LODE RIVER

N

SANDPLACE RAILWAY STATION

CAUSELAND TO SANDPLACE
by road

This is a very easy walk along minor roads displaying a fresh bloom of wild flowers.

Turn left out of Causeland station and pass by Badham Farm continuing ahead alongside the railway in places for the best part of a mile with fine hedgerows bedecked by seasonal flowers. With such lush vegetation it is difficult to see along this section the remains of the old canal adjacent to the railway. Many sections were simply filled in and the railway superimposed on top. More is the pity for a canal and railway side by side would have been rather lovely. Nearer to and beyond Sandplace, however, remains of the canal are more easily discernible.

The road crosses the railway and then at the next junction keep right for the last section to Sandplace station. Come to a junction and turn left for Sandplace and the station.

Unlike Causeland, Sandplace once possessed a siding for the transhipment of sand and agricultural goods. It was never very busy and some writers indicate that sometimes the passenger train picked up trucks from the siding before continuing up the valley. Freight facilities were removed in the 1950s and this left a goods service through to Looe only. This eventually ceased in the mid-1960s.

Sandplace as its name suggests is where sand was brought in up the tidal river to be spread on the land throughout the surrounding areas to improve its quality. This perhaps explains the number of surviving green lanes. They would have originally served as wagonways for transporting sand and lime to the fields and in return bringing agricultural goods to the hamlet and railway.

Sandplace is a tranquil place these days, far enough from Looe to miss the crowds and yet so close to the sea.

Terras Bridge — The remnants of the old canal near Sandplace.

CAUSELAND TO LOOE
by way of Pelynt

This longer walk requires far more time and stamina than most of the others. It is partly along lanes and partly on paths finishing with the lovely section through Kilminorth woods. The path up to Duloe is not easy but those between Pelynt and Looe are obvious.

Turn left out of Causeland station and continue ahead to pass by Badham Farm Holidays. As the road dips to a stream turn right and go through the gate on the left. Follow the field edge on the left up to a point where the field begins to indent and look for a gap which is now filled with brushwood. Cross here to the next field and go slightly left up the field to a gap. Go through it and keep ahead, still climbing, alongside the hedge now to your right. The views behind are well worth a pause.

Proceed through the gateway and then slightly left to another with Westnorth Farm just beyond. Go through the gate and follow the farm track down towards the buildings and around right through to pass by the barn guarded by two gates. This area can get very messy and some ramblers use the narrow path to the right of the iron fencing.

Duloe Church

Continue ahead to a gateway mid-field which you go through and then slightly left towards a stream and a stile hidden in the hedge, just beyond where the hedge cuts back on the left. Cross the stile and walk slightly right to a gateway. Go through it and then go slightly right again to steps leading onto the grass verge of the main road with Duloe church opposite.

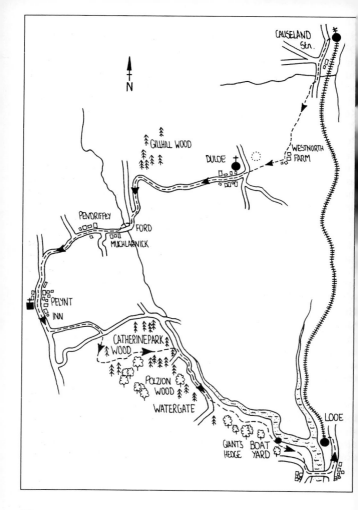

Village Green

If you are stopping for light refreshments turn right for Ye Old Plough inn or the village store. If not cross the road and proceed along the lane signed to the village green. Walk through this and continue ahead along a narrow lane which becomes steeper and rougher by Gillhill Wood. This drops to a junction with excellent views of the West Looe valley. Keep ahead and before the river go right over the stile and then left over the footbridge.

Pelynt

Cross another stile and climb up through the woods to meet a fence which has been lowered for access onto the green lane below. Go right and begin something of a haul up to the few houses of Muchlarnick. At the minor road turn right and walk along this back lane for a good mile to the main road at Pelynt, ignoring turns off. Keep ahead in the village. By now your effort should be rewarded with a stop at The Jubilee Inn, once known more harshly as The Axe but renamed to commemorate Queen Victoria's jubilee. Pelynt is larger than most villages in the area. There are a few shops and by the church is a local information board which is well worth a read.

Hall Rings

Nearby is Hall Rings, a large enclosure with remaining ramparts, dating from prehistoric times. There is also a barrow cemetery near the village where ancient tribal chiefs could have been buried. Neither are unfortunately, open to the public.

Turn first left after the Jubilee Inn along a lane feeding into the West Looe valley once again. However, before too long you come to a junction where you turn right and then sharp left up steps and right as signed. The path passes alongside a garden to a stile which you cross. Then proceed alongside the hedge on the right to another stile just beyond

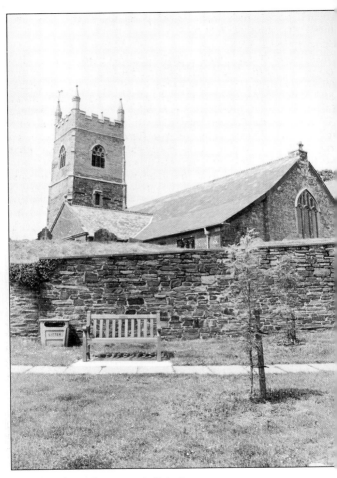

The church and green at Pelynt.

a small pond which seems to be perpetually dry. This leads into Catherinepark Wood.

Catherinepark Wood

Once in the wood avoid following the enticing sunken lane too far but instead turn left over a stile and continue straight ahead down the hill thus avoiding the worn path leading left. The path widens and curves right across the stream and then rises slightly to an opening with three junctions. Go for the middle one which leads gently down hill once again. After the remains of the David Brown tractor the track begins to narrow to a path which goes through older woodland to a stile exiting onto a minor road.

Go straight ahead across the junction and follow this road to Watergate where you turn left and return by way of Kilminorth woods as described in Walk 5. Look out for the irises in the marshy area to the left of the road.

The Jubilee Inn, Pelynt.

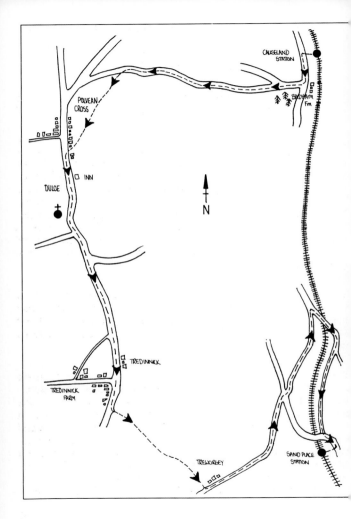

CAUSELAND STATION

POLWEAN CROSS

BRODYAM Fm

INN

DULOE

TREDINNICK

TREDINNICK FARM

TREWORGEY

SAND PLACE STATION

N

CAUSELAND TO SANDPLACE
by way of Duloe

This short ramble follows a steep and narrow lane to Duloe and then along quiet lanes to Sandplace. There are several good views of Looe from Tregorwey.

From Causeland station turn left and then opposite Badham Farm go right and then almost immediately left up a narrow lane to Duloe. This climbs for about a mile high above the valley on your left to a point where Duloe Church can be seen through a gateway. There is a footpath across a field which cuts out some road walking but it is not well marked. Walk diagonally across the field to the far right hand corner, with a row of houses to your right. The right of way is not too clear here now so your nearest exit is by way of the gateway into the next field and then right through the gateway by the village hall.

Tredinnick

This exits on to the main road where you turn left. Follow this past Ye Old Plough inn, the turn to Duloe stone circle and the church on the right. Continue along the right hand side of the road out of the village and as it bends left keep ahead to Tredinnick.

Treworgey

Pass through the hamlet of Tredinnick and turn left along the next track after the turn to Tredinnick Farm. This passes by two houses then curves right with good views of Looe and out to sea. Join the minor road at Treworgey and turn left. This is level at first then descends through woodland to a main road. Go right for a few paces, cross the road with care and go left down a minor road to join another lane by the railway. Go right and at the next junction, over the railway bridge take the lower fork for Sandplace. Turn left for Sandplace station, a delightful spot to finish a ramble.

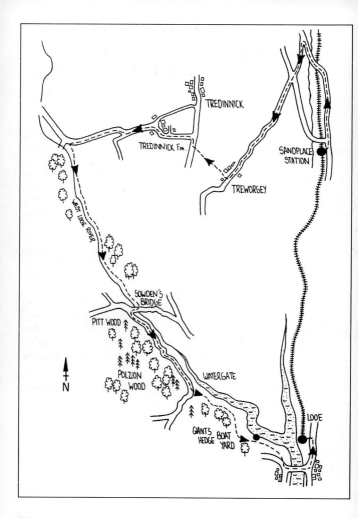

SANDPLACE TO LOOE
by way of the West Looe valley

This ramble involves lane walking into the West Looe valley and a return to Looe by way of Kilminorth woods. The route is obvious but there is one major climb out of Sandplace.

Turn left outside Sandplace station, cross the road just before the bridge and follow this back lane over the railway bridge. A few paces beyond go left up to the main road and cross over with care to join another lane leading up through woodland to Treworgey. Go right here up a track just past the old farmhouse and follow this up through the fields curving left to emerge on the road by some houses.

Green Lane

At the minor road go right and then turn next left to pass by Tredinnick Farm on your right. The track bears left away from the farm buildings and at the next junction take the right fork. This narrow green lane winds its way down to The West Looe. At the bottom, it approaches a gate with a stile and footbridge alongside. However, you turn left and follow the route outlined in WALK FIVE along the West Looe valley to Sowden's Bridge and Watergate. The instructions are outlined from the paragraph marked Tremardart Wood in WALK FIVE.

The walk allows another opportunity to return to Looe station by way of the West Looe estuary.

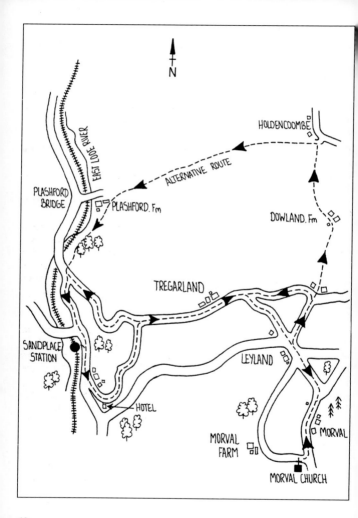

SANDPLACE TO MORVAL CIRCULAR RAMBLE

A short circular walk to Morval Church. Clear tracks and road walking with one climb. There is an alternative route suggested which extends the walk by one mile but in one place this path is less obvious on the ground.

From Sandplace station turn right and follow the road by a row of cottages, the last cottage being the West Looe Valley Crafts and Tea Room, a vital landmark for the thirsty walker as is The Polraen Country House Hotel a few minutes away. Turn left along a minor road at West Looe Crafts climbing past another row of cottages. At the fork turn left again still rising fairly steeply. This must have been one of the early lanes used for transporting sand and lime to the nearby fields of Tregarland. In Sandplace the old lime kilns remain but such activity petered out in the last century. The lane meets a minor road where you turn right.

Tregarland

Pass by a group of houses and farms at Tregarland and take the first turn right to descend to the main road at Leyland by a group of almshouses. Cross the road and turn left to walk by the community hall. Keep ahead along the minor road signed to Morval church and at the next junction turn right. It is a pretty church in a delightful setting, very much part of the Morval estate. Inside the church there is a slate memorial to an earlier local resident Walter Goode, his wife and 12 children.

From here you can either retrace your steps to the main road or some walkers follow the private road through parkland towards Morval Farm then turning right to the old lodge gate at the main road. Go left and before the junction cut off right, cross the road and go up a narrow green lane to a minor road.

The easiest route back is to turn left and follow this route back down the hill to a junction by the railway and river. Turn left here and left again at the main road for the few final steps to Sandplace station.

Alternative Route

For those used to following less well-defined field paths an alternative is to cut across the minor road and proceed ahead along the access road to Dowland Farm. The track passes to the left of the farm and through the left of the barns and then ahead, once again to a gateway in the corner of the field. Do resist the temptation to turn right at two previous gateways. Keep ahead, once again with the hedge now to your left. Go through another gateway and begin to descend down a steep bank to a slight nick in the hedge. There is no stile here so choose the nearest gap to gain access into the field. Head slightly right towards the houses below at Holdencoombe, through the gateway to cross the stream and then at the green lane go left. The instructions back to Sandplace station from here are outlined in the latter paragraphs of WALK EIGHT.

Whichever route you choose this circular walk opens up delightful countryside surrounding the Morval estate.

SANDPLACE TO WRINGWORTHY CIRCULAR RAMBLE

A longer walk through the Morval estate and onto back lanes around Wringworthy. Easy to follow but several climbs.

From Sandplace station follow the walk as instructed in WALK THIRTEEN to Morval Church. However, at the church continue ahead and almost at once Morval House appears also on the right in a fine setting.

Morval House

This ancient Elizabethan homestead dating mainly from the 15th century but with later Tudor and other additions, looks so seductive to the lover of history. It is a private residence, however, and so the walker must be content with a passing glance as the track continues over the brook. Just beyond the pool on the right, bear left at the fork, climbing up between conifers and the occasional rhododendron remnant from earlier landscaping.

No Man's Land

Follow the track up the hill and over the brow as it curves left and leaves the infant woodland. The track comes to a junction by a lodge. The road to your right is the access road to No Man's Land but most ramblers use the road ahead as a shorter route through to the hamlet. At the main road, before the somewhat expanded garage, turn left up a busier-than-expected back road towards the golf course.

Bolventor Lane

Opposite the golf course go left along a minor road in woodland. At the first junction turn right and follow this, known as Bolventor Lane, along a level section at first then down the much narrower route to emerge at Middle

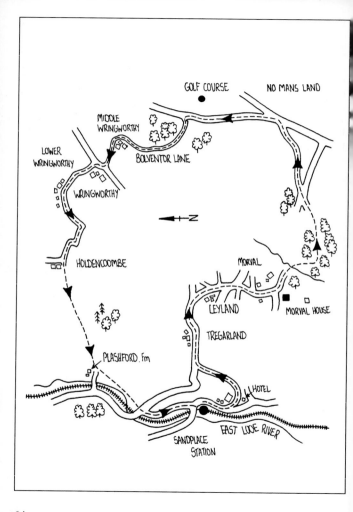

GOLF COURSE

NO MANS LAND

MIDDLE WRINGWORTHY

LOWER WRINGWORTHY

WRINGWORTHY

BOLVENTOR LANE

N

HOLDENCOOMBE

MORVAL

LEYLAND

MORVAL HOUSE

TREGARLAND

PLASHFORD. Fm

HOTEL

SANDPLACE STATION

EAST LOOE RIVER

Wringworthy opposite a farm selling an abundance of country fare.

Go right for a few metres, cross the road and turn left down a minor road to pass Lower Wringworthy and descend further to cross a stream and as the road curves to climb once again, turn left down a green lane. The return route is as described during the last paragraphs in WALK EIGHT. This is, after all, one of the finest remaining lanes open to the walker in this part and is an enjoyable walk time and time again.

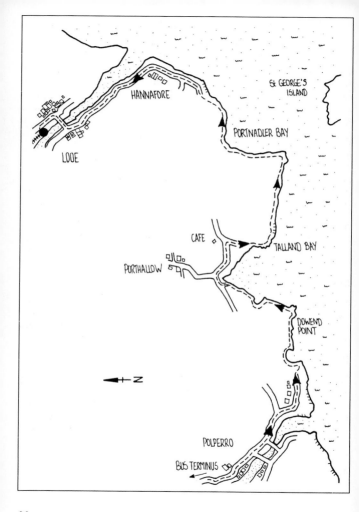

St GEORGE'S ISLAND

HANNAFORE

PORTNADLER BAY

LOOE

CAFE

TALLAND BAY

PORTHALLOW

DOWEND POINT

N

POLPERRO

BUS TERMINUS

WALK FIFTEEN: Approximately 5 miles (8 km)

POLPERRO TO LOOE

This ramble follows the very clearly marked and well worn South West Coastal path to Looe from the historic Cornish port of Polperro, now suffering from a surfeit of tourism. It requires a trip to Polperro by boat or bus. The walk is easy to follow but there are several climbs.

Both the Western National and local bus company, Caradon Riviera Tours, provide a service from the stop between Looe station and the bridge, opposite the health centre. It is approximately hourly during summer months, less frequent during winter. Check along the quayside for details of boat trips to Polperro. For the most part this ramble is waymarked.

Start from the bus terminus on the outskirts of Polperro and turn right to walk down the main street into the village itself. There are, however, motor or horse taxis available for a small sum to take you to the centre of Polperro.

Museum of Smuggling

Follow the signs to the harbour down Talland Street, passing by the Museum of Smuggling. Continue past Shell House and The Old Watch House with the harbour to your right as you climb away from the centre of Polperro.

Polperro Harbour

Not that Polperro is entirely dominated by gift shops selling Piskie trinkets and other momentoes of Cornwall. The area around the harbour is particularly interesting for, until recent decades, the fortunes of this community were very much intertwined with the economic existence of the harbour and smuggling. In fact, the latter was so rife that King George III established a team of customs officers here. Some fishing still takes place and pleasure trips are organised from outside the inner harbour.

As the path forks higher up the hill keep left, signed to Talland Bay, and then at the next junction keep to the lower path, passing by the war memorial at Downend Point and then curving left with the hamlets of Porthallow and Talland Bay coming into sight. The path leads down to a tarmac lane. Go right and when the road bends left keep ahead onto a tarmac track bearing right down to the cove. There is a cafe on the left, which is not always open. The road leads up past toilets and just beyond these, go right. This leads to a car park opposite to 'The Smugglers Bay' Cafe and Restaurant which is usually open for refreshments.

Polperro Harbour from the coastal path.

Talland Bay

Sand from this bay was at one time transported in sea going vessels by way of Looe to Sandplace during the last century. At low tide it is possible to see the colourful rock strata of the bedrock which has been eroded by the sea for millions of years.

St George's Island

Go through the car park on the right and turn left, climbing steeply up the hill now and passing the marker for The Nautical Mile. Naval vessels can be very often seen in the bay testing engines while on speed trials between the two markers. The path is clear along the headland and as it curves around left Looe Island appears. This island is approximately one mile from the coast and is also known as St George's island. Legend has it that St George's was at one time a pirates' den, so much so that a customs post was established there.

Hannafore

The path drops to cross a stream with good views across Portnadler Bay. The houses of Hannafore begin to loom closer. In the final field people have worn a few tracks across but the right of way is along the right hand side to a gateway leading onto the road.

Hannafore Road leads back into West Looe but it is more pleasant to drop down to the path along the seashore by Hannafore Beach. Eventually, you have to return to the road for a short and narrower stretch but there is another little link path descending to river level on your right which leads to the ferry for East Looe. Otherwise, continue along the quayside turning right to cross the bridge and then left for Looe station.

Cornwall's coastline takes some beating and the section between Polperro and Looe could not be finer.

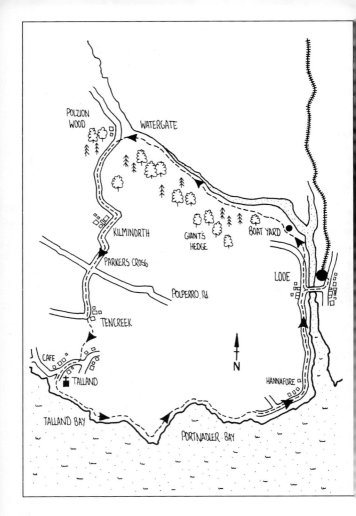

LOOE TO TALLAND BAY CIRCULAR RAMBLE

This walk offers a fine contrast between woodland and coastal walking along obvious paths and lanes. There are climbs throughout so pace yourself accordingly.

Start from Looe railway station. Turn right and walk towards Looe. Cross the bridge and turn right at the far end to pass by an indoor market and amusement arcade. This leads to a walk alongside the old millpond and by The West Looe river on the one hand and the car park on the other. You come to an interpretation board which provides natural history details about Kilminorth woods.

Watergate

Keep ahead along the main track towards the boatyard then just before you reach it cut left, climbing numerous steps, turn right and then step it down towards the estuary. The path curves left and is easy to follow through to Harescombe Lodge at Watergate.

John Wesley

Turn left here and follow the minor road up hill for a considerable distance, passing by Kilminorth cottages and zig-zagging up to the main Polperro road at Parkers Cross. At a nearby crossroads there is a a commemorative plaque to John Wesley, the father of Methodism. Wesley was an inveterate traveller and preached in both Polperro and Looe. Sometimes, as in Looe, he received a poor welcome and had to preach out in the countryside for safety's sake, as not all agreed with his viewpoint.

Tencreek

Proceed across the road with care and walk the short

Stone near Parkers Cross commemorating the visit of John Wesley.

distance to Tencreek. Where the road bends left keep ahead, over the stile and into a field full of caravans and campers. Follow the hedge on your right, to a gap where you cross another stile. In the next field go ahead and follow the field hedge still on your right all of the way around to the far right corner. Cross here the remains of a gate but now amounts to something of a barrier. There are good views of the Nautical Mile and Talland Church.

Once over go right and follow the field boundary on the right, once again, down the field. In recent years the old sunken lane has become overgrown and the right of way as shown on the Pathfinder map is not now possible to follow. The path is directed left at the bottom of the field and then down steps on the right to a minor road.

Talland Church

Go right, passing by Talland church which has a detached tower, presumably used for defensive purposes when the going got tough. A previous priest here gained a reputation for being able to exorcise evil spirits. His most celebrated venture in nearby Llanreath was the exorcism of a ghost coach driven by a man in black and pulled by four headless horses. That must have been quite a task. Continue down the hill and opposite the entrance to The Smugglers Restaurant and Cafe, a welcome refreshment break at this stage, turn left into the car park and then go left again over the stile and uphill. Follow the South Western Coastal Path back to Looe as outlined in the last four paragraphs of WALK FIFTEEN.

What a superb walk of contrasting scenery!

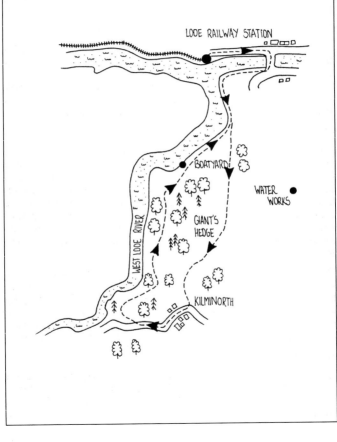

LOOE RAILWAY STATION

BOATYARD

WATER WORKS

GIANT'S HEDGE

WEST LOOE RIVER

KILMINORTH

N

74

LOOE TO KILMINORTH

A short walk through farmland to Kilminorth returning through the woods.

Easy walking but several steady climbs in the first section.

From Looe station make your way to Kilminorth Woods as outlined in the first paragraph of WALK SIXTEEN. From the information board, however, continue ahead, but where there is a turning left to the water treatment works, look for a less well signed path going left into the woods. This leads up a fierce climb to a seat in the woods.

Giant's Hedge

Continue ahead, just on the left of the seat, and then proceed slightly right along this path to a forest track which you cross and then onwards to the remains of an old earth boundary. Nearby are the ramparts of the Giant's Hedge. Legend has it that the devil built it, but a more reasonable explanation is that it was a boundary between a Saxon lord and an ancient British territory. It is thought to date back to the eighth century and stretches about eight miles to the River Fowey.

Once through the old boundary go left and walk up to the stile leading into the field. The next section is not easy to follow for there are no real landmarks at first. Head slightly right up the field, offering fine views of the West Looe river and Looe itself. As you come closer to the top right corner head for a gate on your right in the right hand hedge.

Kilminorth

Go through the gateway and turn right. Follow the old track as it curves gently left downhill to a gateway by a farm. Go through this gate and then through another, almost in sheep pen fashion, as the track exits onto a tarmac minor road. Go right, heading down the hill and passing by Kilminorth Holiday Cottages.

Shortly, the road begins to descend more steeply through the woods. Your way is right through the gateway onto the bridleway. Follow this through the woods. At the other end it leads onto the access road to the boatyard. Go right and retrace your steps alongside the West Looe river to Looe once again.

A BRIEF HISTORY

At first glance the Liskeard and Looe might be described as just another Great Western branch line but this could not be further from the truth. In fact, the Liskeard and Looe line pre-dates its illustrious neighbour by a good few years and is one of that select group of railway companies that began life as a canal company.

Liskeard and Looe Union Canal

The Liskeard and Looe Union Canal opened in 1827 from Terras Bridge, a mile or so up the East Looe estuary to Moorswater, beneath Liskeard. Here tin ore, granite and other goods were transferred from wagons to narrow boats and taken down to sea along what would have been a most tranquil waterway.

Cheesewring and Caradon

The burgeoning demand for these commodities, however, led to the building of a railway from Moorswater to Cheesewring and South Caradon, opened in stages between 1844 and 1846. Trains were horse-worked uphill but descended by gravity when laden. By the late 1850s traffic had reached such levels to warrant the extension of the railway using in many places the line of the canal to Looe. This was opened in 1860. Thus, the lines above Moorswater belonged to the Liskeard and Caradon railway, the line south to the canal company. This was not to be for long for in 1862 the Liskeard and Looe Union Canal company arranged to have its railway operated by the Liskeard and Caradon railway.

Passenger railway

Various extensions took place over the following two decades to meet the demands of the mining industry in the area. In January 1878, the Liskeard and Caradon railway leased the Liskeard and Looe and a year later introduced a passenger service on a formal basis, rather than the erratic use of open wagons for excursions in previous years. At this stage, of course, there was no connection between these railways and the main Cornwall Railway to Truro which passed high above the little company on a spectacular timber trestle viaduct at Moorswater. As mentioned earlier, the stone piers still stand as a reminder of this considerable engineering feat.

A problem relating to any connection with the main line was also the difference in gauge, the Liskeard and Caradon being standard 4'8½" (1435 mm) and the Cornish line being broad 7'0¼" (2140 mm) gauge. Partly as a result of this gauge difference and also to break out of this isolated position the Liskeard and Caradon courted the London and South Western railway and an abortive attempt was made to to join the company's line at Launceston.

A Loop to Coombe Junction

By the 1890s the heyday of the mines and quarries was over and the line's prospects looked less promising. More significantly, the change of gauge on the main line in 1892 led to the revival of a proposal to link with the outside railway world. On the 25th February 1901, the steeply graded and violently curved loop line was opened from Coombe Junction (now just called 'Coombe') to the main line at Liskeard railway station. The Liskeard and Caradon had its own platform at right angles to the main line station, a source of puzzlement to many a traveller ever since. The connecting line was through the Liskeard and Caradon goods yard. A passenger service was introduced on 8th May 1901 and there was, as one would expect, a dramatic rise in passenger traffic to Looe.

Great Western Railway

However, the leasing arrangement went through a complete reversal and the Looe and Liskeard railway took a lease on the Liskeard and Caradon on the same date. This was to be a short lived arrangement for in 1909 the Great Western railway absorbed the Liskeard and Caradon but not, ironically, the Liskeard and Looe line. The latter company simply requested that the Great Western Railway operate the railway on their behalf! In 1923, however, the line became part of the Great Western Empire and after the Second World War a branch line in the Western Region of British Railways.

Quay Closure

Severe decline set in during the 1950s when the line along the quay at Looe, which belonged to The Harbour Commissioners, was closed. Amazingly, the branch survived the Beeching closure programme in the 1960s. The station we see now was set back to allow development alongside the river, otherwise the line remained intact from Moorswater to Looe. One of the key reasons for its survival was without doubt the difficulty envisaged in providing a rail replacement bus in and around the East Looe valley.

Clay trains still use the link line down from Liskeard to Moorswater and this is why the reversal of passenger trains at Coombe Junction requires a changing of the points by the train crew on every trip. The mainstay of the line are two-car diesel multiple units based at Plymouth and throughout the summer British Rail provide a Sunday service as well as the weekday facility. Saturdays are very busy but it is surprising how many people use this facility at other times and although numbers are small, demand still exists from the rural halts along the branch.

For the past thirty years the line has continued, delightfully slow, wonderfully picturesque, the embodiment of what a branch line should be. Ever alongside it lie the remains of its predecessor canal, occasionally glimpsed from the passing train and a reminder of the fascinating history of this unsung branch line.

West Looe Harbour.

IMPORTANT

Since the cover of this book was printed, the telephone numbers for information have changed to 0503 262072 and 0503 262409 respectively. Also please note that 'Pathfinder' maps are 1:25 000 and not 2" to one mile.

In addition, a new information office has opened, the 'South East Cornwall Discovery Centre', Millpool, West Looe, PL13 2AF. Telephone: 0503 262777.

Please note that 'Rambles by Rail 3' will not be available until July 1992 at the earliest, and may be a month or two later.